PANCHATANTRA 2.0
FABLES FOR THE MODERN TIMES

In loving memory of my sister, Swetha—
your innocent smile lives on within me.

And to my mother, Nirmala, with lots of love.

Published by Scholastic India Pvt. Ltd.
A subsidiary of Scholastic Inc., New York, 10012 (USA).
Publishers since 1920, with international operations in Canada, Australia, New Zealand, the United Kingdom, India, and Hong Kong.

For information regarding permission, write to:
Scholastic India Pvt. Ltd.
A-27, Ground Floor, Sigma Centre
Infocity-1, Sector 34, Gurgaon-122001 (India)

First edition: August 2025

ISBN-13: 978-93-5954-152-5

Printed in India at Sai Printo Pack Pvt. Ltd.

PANCHATANTRA 2.0

FABLES FOR THE MODERN TIMES

KARTEEK MANCHALA

Illustrations by
PRIYANKAR GUPTA

democracy (n):

A form of government where citizens have the power to choose their leaders

CONTENTS

A ROAR, A VOTE, AND FALLING MANGOES

'It's been a long day,' Monk sighed, pulling himself up the thick branches of the tall mango tree. Nearby, Wisy the owl perched silently, her wide eyes scanning the ground below. The soft amber light of the setting sun glowed on her beak. Monk the monkey stretched out his arms and legs, preparing for the night as a cool easterly breeze brushed his cheeks, rustling the leaves around him.

'I'm waiting for the mangoes. Last season, I could barely find any,' Monk said with a nostalgic sigh, his eyes scanning the branches in search of budding fruit.

'I hope we get some rain this summer,' Wisy added, her eyes still scanning the ground for mice.

The sun dipped lower, casting the sky in warm golden light. A few low-hovering clouds, which were left behind, caught the fading colours. Resting on the branch and gazing at the horizon, Monk slowly drifted into sleep, and then into a dream.

In the dream, he sailed gracefully across a lake on a small wooden board. Ripples of water formed on either side, creating froth tinged with orange in the soft glow of the setting sun. A light mist wafted onto him, cooling his sunburnt face. He opened his eyes and saw the far shore more clearly, its outline sharpening as the light faded. A gentle spray of water wafted onto his face, delicately peeling away the warmth bestowed by the sun. With each passing moment, he could see the shore on the other side of the lake drawing nearer, its contours outlined by the fading light. The cool breeze filled Monk's body as it entered through his nostrils, refreshing him with each breath. As he approached the centre of the lake, Monk heard his name echoing from behind, 'Monk, Monk!'

Startled, he turned around to see mangoes zipping through the air. As he manoeuvred to evade the fruits aimed at him, Monk lost his footing and tumbled into the lake with a loud splash. When he resurfaced, sputtering and gasping for air, he heard voices calling him from opposite directions.

'Come this way,' a lion roared from one side.

'Come our way,' the rest of the animals pleaded from the other end.

Monk froze, unable to decide which way to go.

He was jolted awake, his dream left incomplete.

As he rolled to his left, he lost his grip on the branch, leaving him dangling by his tail. Rubbing his palms together, he pressed them against his eyes before grabbing the branch again and climbing back up. Half of the sun had already disappeared below the horizon.

'Oh, nice! I didn't get wet,' exclaimed Monk.

'And you didn't wet your bed either!' Wisy chuckled.

'That's a relief, right?' Monk grinned.

'Did you manage to cross the lake this time?' she asked eagerly.

'No, I was really close,' Monk replied, holding up his fingers to show just how near he'd been.

'What stopped you this time?' Wisy asked, curious.

'Mangoes,' Monk said quietly, his face falling as he recalled the sudden interruption in his dream.

Wisy continued her diligent search for mice, while Monk stared into the horizon, lost in thought.

'Are you seeing what I'm seeing?' Monk asked, sitting upright, eyes wide and head leaning forward.

'I can see things far beyond what your ordinary eyes can catch,' Wisy replied without looking up.

'Can you believe it? A tiger being chased by a wolf!' Monk exclaimed.

Wisy remained focused on the ground for her prey, while Monk's gaze followed the action unfolding in the distance. A wolf dashed after a frightened tiger, emerging from the bushes separating the village from the forest. Suddenly, from behind the bushes, a deer burst out, chasing after the wolf.

'This is unbelievable! A deer chasing a wolf—and a tiger!' Monk exclaimed, while Wisy watched calmly.

'Stay tuned for more surprises,' Wisy chuckled.

Then, to Monk's utter shock, a hare appeared with a carrot in its mouth, hot on the deer's tail. Monk could hardly believe what had just unfolded. He scratched his head in confusion.

Monk blinked several times, trying to make sense of the bizarre scene. The roles had completely reversed, and nothing felt right.

'It's kind of nice to see the weaker animals chasing the stronger ones, but...is this the new normal?' Monk asked, bewildered.

'What you're not seeing yet are the humans,' Wisy replied, her voice calm.

'Humans?' Monk exclaimed, his eyes widening in surprise.

Moments later, a group of villagers emerged from the bushes chasing the animals with sticks and slings.

'They're all running away from the humans,' Wisy explained. 'The fastest are at the front.'

As the mystery unravelled, Monk let out a sigh of relief and leaned back against the trunk, resting his hands behind his head.

'Animals sneaking into the village in search of food and then humans chasing them away…this has become the new sport,' Wisy said with a shrug.

'Villagers are coming into the forest to collect wood,

and animals are heading into the village to find food,' Monk chimed in.

Wisy nodded thoughtfully. 'The clouds just hover above the forest, teasing us with a few drops before moving on. The two-year-long drought has only made things even worse.'

Monk sighed, gazing up at the sky. The villagers halted their pursuit as the rabbit, who had stolen carrots from their fields, disappeared into the bushes. Scanning the area for any sign of the sneaky rabbit, the villagers instead spotted Monk perched on the tree and quickly dashed in his direction.

'They're coming after you,' Wisy warned.

'Why?' Monk sat upright, startled by the approaching villagers. 'They recognized you as the one who stole mangoes from their orchard,' Wisy said before taking flight.

'That happened last season. But, how did you know?' Monk asked, bewildered.

'That's for another day; time to escape now,' Wisy replied urgently, flying away.

Monk hastily hopped onto the branches of the adjacent tree, dodging the stones as they whizzed past him. His heart raced as he swung from one branch to another, while the villagers kept slinging rocks in his direction.

'Maybe stealing those mangoes wasn't the best idea!' Monk muttered to himself, leaping to the next tree.

Wisy circled above, watching the chase with a hint of amusement. 'You're quicker than I thought, but they're still gaining on you!' she teased.

'Not helping, Wisy!' Monk called back, barely catching his balance on a thinner branch.

'You might want to pick up the pace,' Wisy chuckled. 'They don't give up easily.'

Monk shot a glance at the villagers before swinging farther into the trees, finally increasing the distance between him and the villagers.

Wisy swooped down and perched nearby. 'That was a great escape.'

'It would've been greater if you had helped,' Monk quipped, still panting.

'Well, I was the one who warned you in the first place,' Wisy replied with a sly grin.

A few days later, the forest council convened an urgent meeting to address the rising number of encounters with the villagers and the dwindling forest resources. Attending were Pyaari the parrot, who had recently escaped from the village fortune teller; Shesha the snake; Shila the bull; Khila the giraffe; Monk the monkey; Gomtha the cow; Ballooka the bear; and other concerned animals. Notably absent was the lion king Maheesha, who was occupied with a hunting expedition alongside his friends.

Shesha, the head of the council, hissed to command attention. 'Listen up, everyone! Please pause your snacking for a moment and focus on the agenda. We need to do something quickly before the villagers catch hold of our tails!'

'What's the agenda again?' Shila asked, looking puzzled as she tried to remember the purpose of the meeting while chewing her snack, 'I seem to have forgotten more than just my lunch!'

All the animals hastily stuffed their mouths with whatever titbits they could grab, their cheeks bulging with food. Gomtha tried to chew her hay, holding her lower jaw still. Monk struggled to manage the juice dribbling down his mouth. Meanwhile, the wild boar made a great effort to bite into the peanuts in slow motion, but the popping shells made surprisingly loud noises with each crunch.

'Greetings, esteemed forest mates,' Shesha hissed, lifting her hood so they would heed her words. 'We urgently gather today to address the pressing challenges facing our beloved Nallamalla Forest. Chief among these concerns are the escalating encounters with humans. We can't keep waiting for Maheesha to decide everything for us. He isn't even here! While we starve and dodge humans, he's out hunting for himself!'

'Well, he's the king, isn't he? That's how it has always been,' Shila the bull chimed in, her mouth full as she chewed noisily.

'But that's not how it works for the humans!' Pyaari the parrot interrupted. 'They choose a new leader every few years. If the leader doesn't do their job, they're free to choose someone else!'

Ballooka the bear froze mid-bite, his eyes wide. 'Humans choose their leaders!' he exclaimed, his voice booming. The fish in his paw had slipped free and was now trying to wriggle back into the lake. 'Do they let the weak ones have a say?'

'Yes, they do. Maybe that's why they seem to thrive while we struggle,' Wisy the owl said, her voice calm. She ruffled her feathers and peered at the group.

'Think about it. Instead of just one leader making all the decisions, what if we all had a say?' Khila the giraffe suggested. 'What if we chose someone who could speak for all of us, not just the strongest?'

'And the tallest!' Shila added with a smile. 'What if we elected someone who understood everyone's needs? Tall, small, fast, or slow?'

'You mean...an election? Like humans do?' Pyaari asked, tilting her head.

'Why not?' Khila replied, bending her neck low to emphasize her point. 'We're all different. If we choose our leader together, maybe we can find solutions that work for everyone.'

Nods of agreement rippled through the gathering. A few animals clapped their paws, while others stamped in approval.

Shesha's eyes narrowed thoughtfully. 'An election…' she hissed. 'How exactly does this election work?' She turned towards Pyaari, who had spent enough time with humans to know their ways.

Pyaari straightened proudly, eager to explain. 'It's simple,' she began. 'Those who want to become the leader announce that they are standing for election. On a designated day, everyone goes to a specific place to vote. Once you vote, you get a blue mark on your finger, so that no one votes twice!'

The animals exchanged intrigued glances.

'And whoever gets the most votes is declared the winner,' Pyaari added.

Deep in thought, Shesha declared, 'Let's hold elections to choose our king. Nallamalla will become a democratic forest.'

The animals cheered, their voices echoing through the forest.

'I roar to differ. You think votes will save us?' Maheesha growled, leaping from behind the bushes, his amber eyes narrowing. 'A lion's roar protects this forest, not chatter and rules!' The king had arrived.

Shesha, unfazed, didn't even hiss in response. 'Let's begin the vote. All in favour of elections, come to my right. If you oppose, move to the left.'

Maheesha strode to the left, watching in disbelief as every other animal moved to the right—except Monk, who stood in the middle, staring straight into Shesha's eyes.

'Monk, I sense indecision. What are you waiting for?' Shesha hissed. 'Why don't you choose a side? Not that it matters now, since we already have enough votes to welcome democracy into the forest.' She spoke with a cool indifference.

'I think we need more time to discuss this,' Monk said thoughtfully. 'Democracy is too big a decision to rush.'

Shesha's eyes narrowed. 'I don't want to wait until another encounter with the villagers. We need a king who works for the betterment of all forest inhabitants,' she snapped.

Maheesha, standing alone on the left, glanced at Monk, hoping he might join him. He shifted uncomfortably, feeling the weight of being the only one opposing. But Monk remained in the middle.

Without further delay, Shesha declared, 'The resolution for democracy has passed. All votes in favour, one against, and one undecided.'

The news of the election spread quickly, creating a wave of excitement throughout Nallamalla. But Maheesha, usually brimming with pride in his strength, felt a growing sense of isolation. He trudged back to the den, his majestic mane drooping. His mighty roar, which once shook the entire forest, now seemed more like a silent sulk. His casual stare could once scatter a herd of elephants, but that day, even a deer passed by without the slightest hint of fear.

As he lay in the stillness of his den, Maheesha closed his eyes and let out a heavy sigh. 'Do they really think they can lead this forest better than me?' he muttered, his deep voice filling the emptiness around him.

'What do they know of strength? Of survival?' But his words echoed softly off the stone walls.

For the first time, an uninviting and unsettling guest crept into his thoughts: doubt.

Could I ever be king again? he pondered as night fell on Nallamalla.

Meanwhile, the idea of choosing their next king filled the woodland creatures with exhilaration. All except one. Monk wasn't so sure. In the quiet of his tree, he wondered if this was truly the best path for the forest. *What if the animals choose someone who only craves power, without caring for the well-being of the forest?* he thought.

CAMPAIGN TIME

One night while hunting, Maheesha cornered a buffalo that had come to drink water from the lake. With his powerful paws, he pinned the buffalo down, his jaws hovering near its neck.

The buffalo, eyes wide with fear, spoke quickly, 'I have some interesting news for you. If you let me go, I'll tell you.'

'Talk fast, before I bite your head off,' growled Maheesha, loosening his grip slightly.

'Doxy the fox is running in the election. He submitted his candidacy to the council today,' the buffalo revealed.

A wave of disbelief washed over Maheesha. He released the buffalo and sank into deep thought. Doxy the fox was well-liked by the animals for his gentle demeanour and kind nature. He always greeted everyone with a smile.

Maheesha couldn't fathom the idea. 'How could a fox become the king of the forest?' he thought bitterly.

The next morning, Maheesha set out to find Monk, scouring every corner of the forest. After a long search, he finally spotted the monkey fast asleep atop a mango tree by the lake.

In his sleep, the monkey had drifted into a strange dream. *He found himself gliding across the lake on a narrow, mango-coloured plank. As he neared the centre, a tree rose from the water, and beneath it lay Doxy the fox, his front legs folded, eyes closed, enjoying the cool morning breeze. A lion approached Doxy, bowed obediently, and dropped a piece of meat before the fox. Doxy leisurely ate while the lion stood by, watching.*

Monk woke up with a jolt. Looking down, he saw Maheesha waiting beneath the tree.

'King Maheesha! What a surprise. Did you bring any meat?' Monk asked, rubbing his eyes, still groggy from his dream.

'What?' Maheesha asked, confused.

'In my dream, a lion that looked like you brought a piece of meat to Doxy,' Monk explained.

'That dream might just become a reality if Doxy is elected as king,' Maheesha replied solemnly. 'But dreams aside, I need your help with the elections. I don't know how any of this works.'

'Are you saying you want to contest the elections?' Monk asked.

'If that's what it takes to become king, then yes,' Maheesha nodded.

'I can be your adviser. First, let's submit your candidacy, and then we'll need to start campaigning for votes,' Monk offered.

'What happens in a campaign?' Maheesha asked curiously as they headed towards the council office.

'You ask for votes,' Monk replied.

'You mean begging? I don't beg. I just take what I need,' Maheesha growled, his voice restless. He let out a powerful roar that echoed through the forest.

Monk grinned and said, 'Campaigning is about telling the animals why they should choose you. We'll highlight your strengths, your vision for the forest, and why you'd make a great king.'

'Why don't we just round them up and force them to vote for me?' Maheesha suggested.

'That won't work,' Monk cautioned. 'The election rules strictly prohibit the use of threats or force. If the committee finds out, you'll be disqualified.'

After a moment of contemplation, Maheesha said, 'Alright, let's campaign.'

Monk leapt with excitement, already envisioning the path ahead. Once they reached the council office, Maheesha formally submitted his candidacy. They returned to the mango tree, where Monk, using his agile tail, began sketching a plan in the dirt. He outlined the key areas of the forest where they should focus their efforts. Together, they crafted a strategy, agreeing to emphasize

Maheesha's strength, his ability to protect the forest, and his commitment to ensuring safety for all the animals.

On a sunny day, Maheesha and Monk set out on their campaign adventure. As they strolled through the forest, they came across a herd of deer peacefully grazing with their heads down. Feeling a little awkward, Maheesha decided to take the lead. With a wide grin, he greeted the deer. Startled by the sight of the lion, the deer bolted in every direction.

'Is something wrong with my smile? Does my breath smell?' Maheesha asked, puzzled.

'They probably think you're here to hunt,' Monk suggested. He sprinted after the fleeing deer, calling for them to stop, but they were too frightened to look back.

Undeterred, they continued their journey and soon encountered a group of hares hopping about, searching for carrots. This time, Monk took the lead, while Maheesha waited behind a bush. Just as Monk began discussing the election, Maheesha stepped out with a big smile. The hares, startled by the sudden appearance of the lion, scurried in all directions.

'Wait! We came to talk about the election!' Monk shouted, but the hares had already disappeared into the bushes.

Disheartened by their second failure, Maheesha and Monk continued walking north. Along the way, they spotted Steady the turtle by the lake. Maheesha decided to try his luck again. He approached Steady and grabbed him with his paws. Instantly, Steady tucked his head inside his shell out of fear.

Maheesha let out a roar in frustration, but the turtle remained hidden in his protective shell.

'I've come to request your vote in the election,' Maheesha said softly, attempting a gentler tone. But Steady refused to emerge. Frustrated by the silence, Maheesha tossed the turtle into the lake. Steady quickly swam away, disappearing beneath the water.

'I don't know whether to be sad that we're failing at this or proud that the animals still fear me,' Maheesha remarked as they continued walking.

'We've only been at it for a couple of hours. Let's not lose hope,' Monk reassured him.

Maheesha and Monk finally reached the edge of the forest, where a few buffalo were enjoying their meal. Spotting a calf, Maheesha promptly approached and asked for its vote. Suddenly, the calf's protective mother appeared from behind and positioned herself in front of it.

Undeterred, Maheesha tried to explain, 'I'm not here to hunt; I've come to ask for your vote in the election.'

The mother buffalo was in no mood to listen to the lion, who had suddenly shown up and frightened her calf. She growled, standing her ground. As tensions rose, other buffaloes began gathering around Maheesha. Despite his efforts to clarify his intentions, he soon found himself surrounded by angry buffaloes. The mother snarled again, her warning clear.

Sensing the danger, Maheesha and Monk decided to make a quick exit before they were completely surrounded. They sprinted away, narrowly avoiding the furious lot. It was a close call as the mother buffalo charged after them, her horns aimed at Maheesha. Monk quickly scrambled up a nearby tree while Maheesha kept running. Fortunately, he escaped by a whisker.

After a while, Maheesha made his way back to the tree where Monk was waiting. He stopped under the tree to catch his breath and let the excitement settle down.

'The buffalo was inches away from me. Can you check if I've got any horn marks? My body's too numb to tell,' Maheesha panted, turning his back to Monk.

'Nothing. You're lucky,' Monk assured him.

'Let's go to the wolves' den,' suggested Monk, once they had regained their energy.

'We're done! I'm not going around begging for votes,' Maheesha roared in frustration.

The campaign had been a disaster, with each attempt being a bigger failure than the previous one. Monk fell silent, deep in thought, trying to figure out their next move. He knew giving up wasn't an option, but convincing Maheesha to keep going seemed like a challenge.

'I'll go alone this time,' offered Monk, sensing Maheesha's growing frustration.

Maheesha stood still, uncertain of how else to ask for votes.

Perched on a nearby tree, Wisy the wise owl, who had been silently observing the scene, finally spoke, 'Why don't you call a meeting?'

'That's a brilliant idea!' Monk exclaimed, his face lighting up like the afternoon sun breaking through the clouds.

Maheesha remained confused, unsure of how a meeting could help his cause. But Monk, quick on his feet, immediately drafted a plan. He outlined how they would gather the animals and present Maheesha's vision for the forest. Maheesha reluctantly agreed.

Monk organized a meeting at the Big Rock for the following day, promising meat and fruits as refreshments for the attendees. He invited all the animals in the forest through Whisparrot—a network run by parrots. The chatty birds carried messages, personal updates, and happenings to every nook and cranny of Nallamalla Forest.

Despite the short notice, many animals showed up. Even Monk was surprised at the turnout. However, as they surveyed the crowd, they quickly realized that only the carnivores had gathered, drawn by the promise of meat. The herbivores were noticeably absent, save for a few. Some avoided the meeting as they feared Maheesha. Others felt that the promise of fruits was not a good enough reason to attend; they were plentiful throughout the forest.

Confused about how to proceed, Maheesha turned to Monk for advice. Monk suggested, 'Let's address the carnivores first. After that, we can think of a strategy to reach out to the rest of the animals.'

Maheesha agreed with Monk's plan. He focused their attention on engaging with the carnivores present at the meeting, hoping to win their support before he could move on to tackling the challenge of reaching the herbivores.

Maheesha ascended the Big Rock, his imposing figure immediately drawing the attention of all the animals devouring the free meat.

'Thank you all for gathering here on such short notice,' Maheesha began. 'I am honoured to stand before you today. As you know, lions have ruled this jungle for generations. We've protected the forest from outside threats and ensured the safety of all its inhabitants. It's unfortunate that I now have to go through an election to continue serving you. But I assure you that even if I'm not elected as your king, I will always be at your service.'

Maheesha paused, taking a deep breath before continuing, 'Today, before all of you, I make this promise: if elected as king, I will ensure you get free meat every day.'

Monk, taken by surprise, rushed to Maheesha to inquire about his unexpected offer. 'Monk, see the number of meat-eating animals who turned up for my speech. That's how I got the idea,' Maheesha explained.

The announcement caused a stir of excitement among the carnivores.

'Does this mean we don't have to hunt anymore?' asked a curious fox.

'Yes, you're correct. No more hunting needed. We'll provide you with the meat,' Maheesha assured him confidently.

The crowd erupted into cheers, thrilled by the promise

of readily available meals. The carnivores eagerly pledged their votes to Maheesha, solidifying their support for his candidacy.

After the meeting, Monk pulled Maheesha aside. 'How exactly are you going to provide free meat? You'll have to hunt day and night to fulfil their demands,' Monk said.

'I don't know. We'll worry about that after the elections. Right now, it feels good that we have the support of the carnivores,' Maheesha said with a casual smile.

'We should call a meeting for the herbivores, too,' Monk suggested.

Maheesha, however, seemed unconvinced. 'Since all the carnivores have pledged their support, why do we need the votes of the herbivores?'

As news of Maheesha's promise spread, the forest buzzed with excitement. The carnivores and omnivores were particularly excited. However, Monk felt uneasy about Maheesha's rash decisions. Disturbed by the unrealistic promises, Monk quietly distanced himself from Maheesha's campaign and returned to his dwelling in the mango tree, concerned about what lay ahead.

Doxy the fox began personally meeting with the animals to request their votes. Upon hearing about Maheesha's free meat offer, Doxy's friends suggested he double the offer to win over more supporters.

Inspired by the success of Maheesha's gathering, Doxy called for his meeting. Surprisingly, only the herbivores showed up; perhaps the carnivores were too busy dreaming about Maheesha's promise of free meat. Undeterred, Doxy addressed the herbivores, promising free fruit for all if elected as king.

'Who will eat fruits except birds and monkeys?' bleated a wild goat.

'If I can just pluck the fruits fresh off the tree, why would I need yours?' remarked a monkey, swinging from branch to branch, toying with the hanging fruits.

'Will you provide fruits that are not in season?' asked a woodpecker, tilting his head with curiosity.

Overwhelmed by the barrage of questions and feeling more like a fruit vendor, Doxy left the meeting scratching his head.

With ten days left until the election, Doxy tirelessly canvassed every corner of the forest, meeting the animals and making his case. Meanwhile, Maheesha, aware that many were still afraid of him, sent the smaller animals to campaign on his behalf.

THE WEIGHT OF A VOTE

As the election approached, excitement rippled through the forest, and animals gathered at the Big Rock to discuss how it would be conducted.

'Do we have to raise our hands?' a curious monkey asked.

'But what if we don't have hands?' hissed a cobra, slithering up.

'Raise your hood then!' the monkey suggested with a grin.

'We'll just flap once for Maheesha, twice for Doxy!' a parrot joked, swooping down.

'What about splashing mud once for Maheesha and twice for Doxy?' suggested a pig.

'In that case, we will get a free mud bath on election day!' quipped a crane hovering above them.

The animals roared with laughter, picturing a muddy, chaotic election full of flapping wings, slithering cobras, and buffaloes stomping around to get their choice noted. Yet, amid the fun, no one really knew how the election would be conducted, which only made it more intriguing.

Maheesha and Doxy intensified their efforts, trying to attract last-minute voters. Maheesha, aiming to secure support from the carnivores, cleverly chose a chunk of meat as his campaign symbol, hoping to sway their vote with his promise. Meanwhile, Doxy, confident in his charm and reputation, boldly opted for his face as his symbol, trusting his popularity would work in his favour.

The forest council meticulously prepared for the big day, setting up two bags behind a large screen made from palm leaves—one for Maheesha and one for Doxy. Each animal would cast their vote by dropping an almond into the bag, which represented their preferred candidate. Squirrels, assigned with the crucial task of collecting almonds, worked tirelessly day and night to ensure there was enough for the entire election. As the election approached, the anticipation mounted, setting the stage for a fierce contest between Maheesha and Doxy.

When the long-awaited day arrived, the entire forest gathered at the Big Rock, the omnivores and carnivores especially eager to cast their votes. They formed orderly lines, excited to drop their almonds into the bags.

'These almonds are not for eating. I repeat, these almonds are not for eating. Please drop them in the bags of the candidate of your choice!' Shesha, the snake, announced loudly, slithering around the crowd to ensure there was no confusion.

A team of squirrels stood by, ready to refill the almond supply if needed. As the crowd grew larger, the council had to scramble to prepare extra bags to accommodate the overwhelming number of voters.

As the sun began to set, the council hurried to complete the voting process. They made sure every animal that came had a chance to cast their vote. With the ballots finally collected, the first election of Nallamalla drew to a close. The exhausted council and the squirrels exhaled a collective sigh of relief.

As the voting ended, a wave of anxiety swept through the forest, particularly among those who had not cast their votes. Maheesha, consumed by nervousness, paced restlessly within his den throughout the night, forgoing his usual hunting routine as he awaited the results. Meanwhile, Doxy remained beside the Big Rock, his gaze fixed on the horizon as he anxiously awaited the outcome. The woods seemed to hold their breath, with every rustling leaf and whispering wind adding to the palpable tension.

The next morning, Monk remained deeply asleep on the high branches of the mango tree. The sunlight was yet to pierce the thick veil of cloud cover blanketing the sky. The mist clung stubbornly to the leaves, unmoved by the cool breeze from the nearby lake. Amid this tranquil scene, Monk drifted into a dream.

Monk glided gracefully across the lake on a small wooden board. Ripples fanned out from either side, forming frothy patterns that sparkled like stars, as if they were oozing out of the water only to fall back into the lake. A gentle spray of water wafted onto his face, delicately peeling away the warmth of the sun. The Big Rock on the shore grew larger with each passing moment. Monk shielded his eyes from the glare bouncing off the rock and continued his journey. As he neared the lake's centre, a distant voice echoed from behind, calling his name, 'Monk, Monk!' He fought the urge to turn back, focusing on the journey ahead. Suddenly, a smiling Maheesha emerged from the lake, speeding towards him with surprising grace. Before Monk could even react, Maheesha collided with him, sending them both tumbling into the water. In an instant, almonds began to rain down from the sky, falling all around them, bouncing off the water's surface with soft plops.

Monk woke up with a start to find Wisy the owl perched beside him. 'What was it this time?' she inquired.

'It's almonds,' Monk responded, searching beneath the tree.

'Come on, it was just a dream. No almonds fell on you, and none are left on the trees. Every piece was collected for the elections,' Wisy reassured him.

'It felt so real,' Monk sighed.

'Let's go to the Big Rock, it's counting day. We'll find out who our next king is,' Wisy urged.

'I'm not interested,' Monk muttered, attempting to return to sleep.

'Come on! It will be fun. We'll see how they count the almonds,' Wisy teased, nudging him with her wing.

Monk reluctantly gave in. He got up, stretched, and lazily prepared to head to the Big Rock.

'Can we eat the almonds after the votes are counted?' asked Chikur, a young squirrel who had been waiting at the Big Rock since morning.

'We don't know what the council plans to do with them yet. Let's wait and see,' replied the chief squirrel.

'It's not fair; we are the ones who collected the almonds, and now there are none left on the trees,' Chikur complained, kicking the dirt.

The chief shot an angry glance at Chikur as the forest council brought the vote bags filled with almonds from the a small cave behind the Big Rock, where buffalo guards had kept watch day and night. They placed them before the eager animals who were waiting to know the results of the election. Maheesha and Doxy exchanged anxious glances as the council deliberated on how to determine the candidate who had received more almonds.

Wisy and Monk also arrived and settled down in a nearby tree. The tree was abuzz with chatter from the birds, making it difficult for Monk to hear anything from the council, who had formed a close circle around the bags.

'Silence!' Monk shouted, looking up at the noisy birds. The birds paused for a moment, glanced at Monk, and resumed their prattle. Monk tried to concentrate on the conversation on the ground when a bird accidentally dropped its 'blessing' on Monk's head.

'Apologies, your voice startled me, and I could not hold any longer,' the bird remarked sheepishly as Monk shot an angry look at it. The bird hastily retreated to a higher branch.

'Are you sure almonds rained on you in the dream? Maybe it was bird poo,' Wisy quipped, barely able to contain her laughter.

Monk shot a glare at her, but Wisy just kept laughing.

'Can you hear anything?' Monk asked, wiping his head with a leaf.

'I don't hear anything, but it looks like they're figuring out how to count the almonds,' Wisy replied, as she flew and perched on Gaja the elephant.

'We should count how many almonds each candidate

received. Who's good at counting?' Khila the giraffe asked, her long neck swivelling as she looked around.

No one stepped forward, each animal awkwardly glancing at their neighbour, hoping someone else would volunteer.

'Counting could take days. Judging by all the anxious faces, I doubt they'll give us that much time,' Gomtha said, still munching her breakfast lazily.

'We don't even have a number system for counting this many almonds,' added Wisy, understanding the situation. 'Why don't you weigh them instead?' she suggested.

The animals exchanged curious glances, murmuring among themselves. Wisy's suggestion seemed like a straightforward and practical solution to count the votes. The forest council felt a wave of relief.

Quickly, they devised a plan, asking Gaja the elephant to gather a sturdy bamboo stick. The almonds received by each candidate were then transferred to a larger bag. Each bag was fastened to one end of a bamboo stick using banyan tree roots.

Gaja stepped forward and slid his trunk under the stick, positioning it precisely at its midpoint. Then, he began to lift it gently. As he raised it higher, the stick gradually tilted to one side. Maheesha's bag, heavier than Doxy's, came closer to the ground. Many of the animals gazed silently at

Gaja, unsure of what the tilting bamboo stick meant. They exchanged puzzled glances.

Maheesha and Doxy, standing by their bags, waited with bated breath, unsure of what the tilt signified.

'What does this even mean?' asked a deer, squinting at the tilting stick.

Shesha, the snake, slithered onto the Big Rock and declared, 'Maheesha's bag is heavier.'

She paused for a moment, expecting applause, but all the animals remained silent, looking confused.

Undeterred, Shesha continued, 'Maheesha has received more votes.'

Suddenly, the crowd erupted into applause, their cheers reverberating throughout the forest.

'On behalf of the forest council, I declare Maheesha the winner, the first elected king of almonds—sorry, Nallamalla. Congratulations to Maheesha,' Shesha announced, quickly correcting herself as she slithered down from the rock.

Maheesha's supporters rejoiced, breaking into a wild dance. Amidst the celebration, they brought forth the almond bag and ceremoniously cut it open over Maheesha's head. He curled with joy as almonds rained down upon him. The squirrels watched in disbelief as some of the almonds became dirty and others rolled into the lake.

'Don't worry, I saved you a few,' the chief squirrel reassured Chikur, patting him fondly.

The next day, Maheesha arrived at his swearing-in ceremony in a grand procession. All the animals gathered at the Big Rock. Wisy was perched on the same tree as the counting day, but she couldn't persuade Monk to come.

Maheesha, accompanied by his followers, was all smiles as he waited for the ceremony to begin.

With his right paw raised, he solemnly declared, 'I, Maheesha, do earnestly swear to uphold the rights of all residents of the jungle, to defend the sacred right to nap in the sun and to hunt under the moon's glow. I pledge to treat all creatures with fairness and respect—except during the hunt. May you all be blessed with bountiful feasts.'

'Free meat, free meat!' chanted a few enthusiastic animals from the back.

'Yes, I remember the promise,' Maheesha grinned.

Addressing the gathering with humility and grace, Doxy said, 'My fellow jungle mates, I accept defeat with dignity. I'll admit, it stings a bit, like a thorn in my paw. But fret not, my dear supporters! Though our spirited campaign couldn't *outfox* the majestic Maheesha, we'll return even stronger.

'To Maheesha, I offer my sincere congratulations. May your reign be as grand as your mighty mane!

'As for me, though I may not wear the crown, I remain here for you all—except when I'm hunting, of course. Feel free to come to me, unless I'm catching up on sleep!'

And with a mischievous smile, Doxy added, 'I call upon the squirrels to step forward and claim my bag of almonds. They rightfully belong to you, as you worked so hard to gather them. Besides, my teeth aren't cut out for cracking those shells!'

Chikur clapped joyfully, drawing the attention of everyone around.

To conclude the ceremony, a group of woodpeckers carried in a wooden crown, intricately carved and studded with a single gem at its centre and placed it over Maheesha's head. It was adorned with rare seeds, jasmine blossoms, and vibrant bougainvillea flowers gathered from across the forest. The elephants raised their trunks and blew loud trumpets, and the monkeys played drums. The jungle celebrated, with animals cheering and dancing as the sound of trumpets, and drums and singing of birds filled the air. It was a spectacle like no other, a fitting conclusion to the first-ever election at Nallamalla Forest.

ANIMAL FARMS

The festivities continued well into the night. The animals danced wildly to the energetic rhythm of the instruments. Monkeys swung from branches, flipping mid-air as they cheered. Bears stomped their feet in a clumsy but joyful dance. Deer ran gracefully in circles, parrots flapped their wings to the beat, and even the usually serious buffaloes joined in, swaying their tails side to side. Maheesha's heart thumped in sync with the beat of the drums. He stood tall, his chest swelling with pride as he adjusted the wooden crown on his head.

After the night of celebration, Maheesha returned to his den, tired but exhilarated. He paused for a moment, recalling the day's events with a contented smile. He remembered Shesha's announcement, the almonds raining over him, and the birds placing the wooden crown on his head. He yawned, feeling his head droop lower and lower. Forcing his eyes open, he reached up and checked the top of his head. The crown was still in place. The early morning sunshine fell on the shiny gem embedded in the crown, casting a brilliant light across the entire den. Unable to stand any longer, he collapsed onto the floor and drifted into a deep sleep, the smile still adorning his face.

From then on, Maheesha proudly displayed the crown upon his head as he roamed the forest, checking it periodically. He even wore it while hunting.

As king, Maheesha didn't get any special food privileges—he still had to hunt for his meals like every other animal. A few days later, on one of his hunting trips, Maheesha couldn't catch a single prey. Every time he tried to pounce, the animals seemed to scatter away well before he could make his move. This happened again and again, leaving the mighty hunter both frustrated and confused.

Determined to find out what was wrong, Maheesha shifted his focus to smaller animals. Finally, he managed to corner a little rabbit under his paw.

'How did you know I'm coming for you? Am I too loud?' Maheesha growled, his voice rumbling like distant thunder.

The rabbit quivered in fear but stayed silent.

'Speak up! I'll let you go if you tell me the truth,' Maheesha offered impatiently.

'You have a tracking device on your head,' the rabbit squeaked, daring to smile a little.

'What nonsense!' Maheesha scoffed, but he instinctively reached up to touch his crown. 'Where?'

'The stone at the centre,' the rabbit explained, its voice steadier now. 'It glows brightly, especially in the dark. That's how we all know you're coming.'

Startled, Maheesha removed his crown and examined it carefully. He frowned as he realized that the rabbit was right—the gem at the centre emitted a faint light.

'I see…' Maheesha muttered, sighing heavily. He released his paw, letting the rabbit scramble away into the bushes without looking back.

Standing alone in the clearing, Maheesha stared at his crown. Finally, it was clear why his prey had always been a step ahead.

From that day forth, Maheesha left the crown in his den whenever he went hunting. Without the bright gem revealing his arrival, he was able to again move quietly and catch his prey with ease.

Maheesha remained ever vigilant, keeping watch over Nallamalla Forest. When he wasn't hunting, he spent his time protecting the forest from external threats and settling disputes over hunting territories.

One evening, as Maheesha was preparing to go out for a hunt, he noticed two tigers standing outside his den. Curious, he stepped out and asked, 'Do you want to join me for hunting?'

Instead of responding, the tigers held up a placard that read: 'Free Meat Now!'

Annoyed, Maheesha chased them away. But the next day, a few bears showed up with the same demand. As the days passed, more and more carnivores began gathering outside his den. An unease gripped the animals. What started as hushed whispers soon turned into clusters of gossip. The gossip grew louder until it blossomed into lively chatter that reached every corner of the jungle.

The carnivores eventually approached Maheesha in groups, reminding him of his promise of free meat. But Maheesha remained aloof, refusing to address their demands.

The animals, frustrated by his silence, began staging demonstrations outside Maheesha's den, waving his election symbol above their heads. What started as a small, silent gathering soon snowballed into a full-blown protest. The carnivores took turns holding signs and chanting, 'Free meat! Free meat!' It lasted all day and night. To disrupt

Maheesha's peace, they even blared loud music while he tried to sleep.

As their frustration mounted, the animals grew bolder. They began shadowing Maheesha on his hunting trips, deliberately scaring off his prey before he could strike.

'You've come all this way. Why don't you hunt for yourselves?' Maheesha growled, his patience wearing thin.

But the animals didn't budge. They continued their tactics, alerting every creature Maheesha tried to approach. Their relentless interference made hunting nearly impossible, and life increasingly difficult for the king.

Relenting to their demands, Maheesha convened a meeting with his council of ministers. After much debate and discussion, they devised a new plan to address the unrest. Maheesha established an animal hunting squad made of volunteers eager to take on the challenge. To bolster their ranks, he recruited experienced hunters from neighbouring, less prosperous forests, promising them free food in exchange for their service. The squad's primary task was to hunt and procure meat for the carnivores of Nallamalla.

The hunting squad employed a range of techniques—net traps, coordinated ambushes, and surprise attacks—to capture unsuspecting prey within the forest. Once caught, the animals were brought back, and their meat distributed to those carnivores who requested it.

Word spread quickly, and more carnivores began approaching Maheesha, demanding their share of free meat. As demand surged exponentially, the hunting squad struggled to keep up. It soon became clear that relying solely on hunting wasn't sustainable. In response, King Maheesha issued an order to establish farms to hold and breed the captured animals.

Within weeks, farms for hens, ducks, goats, rabbits, cows, and bulls were set up across the forest. These farms aimed to ensure a steady and sustainable supply of meat, reducing pressure on the hunting squads and stabilizing food distribution for Nallamalla's carnivores.

However, the conditions within these farms were far from ideal. Captured animals were crammed into small, confined spaces with no room to move and no hope of escape. The establishment of these farms left many herbivores disheartened, and they lived in endless fear of being caught.

Meanwhile, the hunting squads operated relentlessly. No time or place was safe from their reach. They employed new, far more ruthless methods—paw traps, cages, and even snares made of banyan tree roots—to capture the herbivores, no matter how small. The constant threat of being cornered by the squad spread panic throughout Nallamalla Forest, forcing the herbivores to always be on high alert. Whether foraging for food or searching for water, they knew they could be taken at any moment, adding to their anxiety.

Feeling neglected and unheard, a group of herbivores banded together to voice their grievances to King Maheesha.

'O mighty king, we humbly seek to bring our grievances to your attention,' pleaded a deer, bowing his head with his antlers lowered in a show of respect.

'The free meat policy has taken a heavy toll on us. The hunting squad is everywhere,' he continued, voicing the fears and frustrations shared by many of the herbivores.

A duck stepped forward next, her voice trembling but determined. 'The hunting squad is even in the lake! They are capturing us indiscriminately and throwing us into those enclosures. We are residents of this forest, too. As king, you have a responsibility to protect us as well.'

'Did you vote for me?' Maheesha asked, narrowing his eyes.

'Of course, yes! We all voted for you,' the duck stuttered nervously.

'I don't think so. You all voted for Doxy,' Maheesha countered, his voice tinged with suspicion.

A cow stepped forward, chewing thoughtfully before speaking. 'We may have voted for Doxy, but we're still inhabitants of the Nallamalla Forest. Please, disband those animal farms and dismiss the hunting squad before we go extinct.'

Maheesha waved his paw dismissively. 'You can order meat if you want. I'll inform the food minister.'

'You know, we don't eat meat. How can we eat it if our tummies aren't made for digesting it?' asked a monkey, scratching his head in confusion.

Despite the herbivores' earnest pleas, Maheesha remained silent and aloof. His thoughts were elsewhere—focused entirely on his upcoming re-election. *I already have the carnivores' votes to win*, he thought, dismissing their concerns. *Why should I care?*

The animals left crestfallen, their hopes dashed and their pleas unanswered. Unsure of what to do next, they slowly dispersed into the forest, tails drooping and heads bowed.

'Watch out for the hunting squad on your way home!' Maheesha joked, a grin spreading across his face.

As time passed, the number of farms grew by leaps and bounds, each feeding the growing demands of the hungry carnivores. The once-tranquil landscape of Nallamalla Forest became dotted with these morbid enclosures, their wooden fences and cages casting long shadows over the meadows that used to be green and open.

Many animals that were previously omnivores now registered themselves as carnivores, eager to reap the benefits of the king's 'free meat' policy.

When the frogs began requesting insects, an insect farm was promptly set up to cater to their needs. Soon after, the snakes demanded frogs, leading to the creation of a separate frog farm. Not long after that, the eagles requested snakes, prompting the construction of yet another compound filled with wriggling serpents. In the end, the insects ended up feeding on the remains of dead eagles, completing the food cycle.

A few months passed. The long-awaited festival of summer solstice had arrived in Nallamalla Forest. Animals buzzed with excitement as relatives from neighbouring forests travelled to join in the celebrations. The sun shone brightly overhead, casting a warm glow over the woods and filling the air with a sense of joy and anticipation. The monsoon had not arrived yet. Amid this lively atmosphere, a group of wolves strolled through the forest, their movements unhurried and carefree.

Along their path, the wolves encountered a bunch of hares hopping by. One of the visiting wolves, Rolf, who was from a neighbouring forest, immediately grew excited at the sight.

'Look, they're not afraid of us. No fear in their eyes. Let's attack them and have a feast!' Rolf howled eagerly, already springing forward.

But his host, Todel, stepped in calmly and blocked his path. 'Relax, my friend. Do you really want a hare for lunch?' he asked, with a gentle smile.

'Yes, let's hunt,' Rolf insisted, taking another stride towards the hares. But to his surprise, the hares remained completely unfazed. They glanced at the wolves with mild curiosity before leisurely continuing on their way, nibbling on leaves.

Todel chuckled and placed a paw on Rolf's shoulder. 'There's no need to hunt here. We get free meat,' he said reassuringly. 'I'll order a hare for you.'

Rolf blinked in confusion. 'Order a hare?'

'Yes,' Todel grinned. 'We're a democratic forest, and our king promised free meat to all carnivores. There are special farms just for this purpose. I've already arranged for hares to be delivered for lunch.'

Rolf stared at him, stunned. 'No more hunting?'

'No more hunting,' Todel confirmed with a knowing smile.

Hearing this, the other wolves burst into laughter and howled in unison, the sound echoing through the woods. The hares looked back, eyes narrowing with disdain, then continued their way, leaving the wolves behind.

IN THE LAP OF A HUNTER

In the heart of Nallamalla Forest, lies an enclosure of ancient trees called Whispering Woods. The trees were so thickly intertwined that sunlight could only peek through when a tree bent to murmur its secrets to a neighbour. With each gust of wind, the beams of light swayed like dancers to the soothing melodies played by the wind wafting through the dense canopy of leaves.

In this enchanted grove lived a hare named Hari. His friends seemed to orbit around him, drawn by his uncanny ability to sniff out hidden roots and sense danger before it surfaced. Whether foraging along the forest's edge, dodging the shadows of circling hawks, fleeing from swift-footed foxes, or racing each other through dense bushes, they always stuck together.

But life in the Whispering Woods was changing. King Maheesha's rule was at its height. Carnivores began to outnumber herbivores, and the animal farms expanded daily. Driven by rising demand, the hunting squad set their sights on hares and rabbits, rounding them up by the dozens and putting them into farms. For Hari and his friends, the forest that was once their playground had become a place of eternal vigilance and fear.

One afternoon, when the sun was high in the sky, Hari and his friends went wandering through the woods near their grove, foraging for food. Hari's ears twitched as he caught the faint rustling of leaves nearby. He froze, then motioned for his friends to stop and crouch low. They exchanged fearful glances, trembling as they huddled close together.

'Could it be the hunting squad?' Hari wondered, his heart pounding as he scanned the surroundings.

Hari signalled to his friends to spread out. Suddenly, a wooden cage came swinging out from a nearby bush, crashing towards them. Swiftly, the hares darted in different directions, racing for cover. Hari dashed into a thick patch of shrubs and peered out, frantically looking for his friends.

A terrified squeal pierced the air as one hare struggled. His tail was caught under the cage. Hari's ears drooped down. Before he could react, the hunting squad swooped in, lifted the trapped hare and tossed it into a larger cage. They leapt forward, searching for the other hares that had escaped.

Hari took off south, sprinting as fast as his legs could carry him, the predators hot on his heels. A wave of guilt washed over him—he couldn't save his friend. But there was no time to look back. He darted around trees and bushes, expertly weaving through the dense forest, even diving under fallen trunks to throw off his pursuers. The cage was swung at him several times, narrowly missing each time as he twisted and turned around the trees. Gasping for breath and unsure of where to go, Hari continued to head in the direction of the village.

As he neared the village, Hari glanced back over his shoulder. The hunting squad was nowhere in sight. Feeling relieved, he kept running until his legs felt like they would give out. Finally, he spotted a dense thicket and ducked inside. His body ached, and before he knew it, exhaustion swept him away into deep sleep.

By the time Hari woke, the sun was inching beneath the horizon. He looked around for his friends, but the woods were silent. There was no sign of them.

I hope they're safe, wherever they are, Hari thought.

Hari stretched, his limbs stiff from all the running. His stomach started rumbling, demanding food. With little energy that is left, Hari sniffed the surroundings. A sweet, earthy aroma caught his attention. He followed it with his nose twitching, and to his delight, he spotted a red, juicy carrot lying on the ground, freshly plucked. He stretched his front paw to grab the carrot. Just as his paw brushed the carrot's smooth skin, a wooden cage came swinging down from above, crashing into the ground. Hari's heart leapt—a trap! Hari quickly pulled his paw and bolted away, his ears reaching towards the sky, as he ran.

Now they've started using baits! Hari thought bitterly, his heart pounding as he sped through the forest. The crimson twilight slowly merged with the darkness that began to engulf the forest. Despite the fast-fading light, Hari kept running, eyes fixed on a faint glow in the distance—a street lamp at the village's boundary.

Hari was nearing the village's border when he suddenly stepped onto a soft bed of leaves. Before he knew it, the leaves caved in. He slipped through the cracks, landing with a thud on the hard, damp ground below. Dazed, he looked around and realized he had fallen into a deep pit. That road along the village had similar traps to capture elephants, lions, and other wild animals.

It was pitch-black inside. With wide eyes, Hari tried to peer into the darkness, but it felt as if a thick blanket covered his eyes. Despite being deep underground, the pit felt safer compared to the danger of the hunting squad lurking above. As he caught his breath, he decided it was best to wait until morning to search for a way out. Hari closed his eyes (even though it made no difference in the darkness), and soon, he was snoring.

The next morning, sunlight filtered through the gaps between the shrivelling leaves, warming Hari's face. He stirred awake, his body still sore from all the running the day before. Blinking against the bright light, Hari's eyes widened as he noticed a human sitting in the opposite corner of the pit.

The man was awake, watching him quietly. Hari's ears stiffened against his back, and he froze, staring back at the stranger.

They locked eyes for a few moments. Instinctively, Hari scanned the pit for an escape route, but it was too deep. There were no footholds or branches to help him climb out. When he turned back to the man, he noticed a gentle smile on his face, as if to say he had already tried and failed. Throughout the morning, they sat in silence, exchanging glances. They found a strange comfort in their shared confinement.

As afternoon approached, Hari glanced upwards, straining to hear any sign of his friends. However, all he heard was the gentle rustling of the swaying trees and the cheerful chirping of birds. A wave of dizziness washed over him, and he struggled to sit upright. It had been an entire day since he'd last eaten. Though he had nibbled on a few berries and dry leaves scattered on the floor of the pit, they hadn't been nearly enough to calm his rumbling stomach.

As Hari nibbled on the last of the berries he had salvaged, the man set a small bag in front of him and began to open it. Hari felt a surge of fear and instinctively retreated into the farthest corner of the pit, with his ears bent backwards.

Is the man going to pull out a gun or a knife? Is he going to cut me up? Hari's thoughts raced through his mind.

But to his surprise, the man retrieved a packet of food from the bag. Hari's expression shifted from one of fear to eagerness. Cautiously, he inched forward, eyes fixed on the packet, wondering what was inside.

Inside, there were roasted peanuts. The man opened the packet and popped a few into his mouth, savouring each bite. Hari watched with anticipation, his nose twitching as the scent of the peanuts filled the earthy air. He waited, hoping the man might offer him some. But nothing of the sort happened. After a while, the man picked up a bottle of water and drank again, without sparing a thought for Hari. Disappointed, Hari nibbled on a few blades of grass he found in the pit and eventually drifted off to sleep with an almost empty stomach.

The next morning, Hari woke up with a start, eyes wide as bright orange carrots rained down into the pit. They quickly piled up around him, about to drown him. He scrambled up to stay above them. Suddenly, a carrot smacked him on the head, and he woke up with a start.

Hari blinked and looked around. There were no carrots—just the same empty pit. He touched his head but felt no bump. It had all been a dream.

Hari's stomach rumbled the moment he woke up. Alas, there was nothing to eat. Then he remembered the packet of peanuts in the man's bag. Gathering some courage, he cautiously approached the sleeping man. Every time the man let out a loud snore, Hari jumped back, mistaking it for a growl. Realizing the noise was harmless, he gathered all his courage and approached the man. Sniffing around, Hari located the bag, tucked right under the man's head, serving as a pillow. He carefully tried to tug it out, but it wouldn't budge.

The man woke up to the sound of Hari sniffing around. Startled, Hari darted back to the corner, trembling in fear. The man hugged the bag tightly. He then closed his eyes and drifted back to sleep. Hari's throat was parched, and his stomach ached with hunger. He watched helplessly as the man eventually woke up, stretching his arms and legs with a yawn.

The man opened his bag, extracted the packet, and tossed it away immediately. Ants were crawling all over it. A few began creeping up his hand. He shook them off, watching as the ants swarmed over the scattered peanuts and began carrying them away, one by one. The man watched helplessly. With a sigh, he picked up the bottle and drank the last few sips of water.

Hari, light-headed from hunger and thirst, slipped into a restless sleep while the man sat, unmoved by his plight and humming softly.

Hari lay curled up in a corner, shivering in his sleep. Dark clouds had gathered overhead. A low rumble of thunder echoed in the distance, growing louder as the storm drew closer. Then, a few cold drops of rain splattered onto Hari's head, waking him up. It started raining heavily, and large droplets trickled through the leaves of the branches covering the pit. Desperate for water, Hari drank the rainwater pooling around him, gulping down to fill his empty stomach. He also nibbled on a few soggy leaves that had fallen from above, but it wasn't enough to ease his hunger.

It rained enough to create a puddle of water at the bottom of the pit. The man's side of the pit was lower, and water began to pool around him. Hari glanced over and gestured for the man to join him on the higher, drier ground. The man quickly moved over before his clothes got soaked. They trembled in silence as a chilly breeze swept through the pit. Needing warmth, Hari cautiously cuddled up against the man's side. Surprised but understanding, the man wrapped an arm around the little hare. Together, they huddled close, sharing what little warmth they had, waiting patiently for help to arrive.

The air grew colder as the sky stayed overcast and dark. Hari began making distress calls, hoping his friends might hear him if they were nearby. Hearing the sounds, the man tilted his head upwards and started making strange noises of his own. Soon, it turned into a playful competition to see who could make the loudest noise.

The darkness slowly blanketed the pit. Hari and the man continued making distress calls in their unique ways. Both were hungry and tired, their voices growing hoarse. Just as they were about to give up, a faint, familiar sound echoed through the trees.

Hari's ears perked up. He recognized that call—it was one of his friends! He called out again, and a series of answering calls floated into the cold, dark pit. They were growing louder and coming closer. Hari's friends peeked through the gaps in the leaves to find Hari cuddled with a man. They indicated to Hari not to be afraid, assuring him that they would find a way to get him out.

One of the hares quickly ran to the nearby fields and returned with a carrot. He carefully dropped it into the pit, which splashed into the puddle of water. Hari picked it up and was about to take a bite, but stopped. He glanced at the man, who watched him silently. Hari's paw trembled as he stretched it out, offering the carrot to the man. The man's eyes widened in surprise. Despite his hunger, Hari was willing to offer his food to the man. Deeply moved by the hare's selflessness, the man's eyes moistened with tears. He shook his head gently and motioned for Hari to eat. After a few moments, more carrots fell into the pit, landing beside them. The man picked them up, rinsed them in the puddle, and ate one while passing the others to Hari, who had already finished the first one. They sat there, munching the carrots eagerly, while Hari's friends watched from above, surprised at the bond between man and hare.

The next morning, Hari's friends returned with a few more carrots and resumed searching for ways to get him out of the pit. The man began making signs with his hands, moving them up and down in a wide arc, before narrowing them as they came down. Hari's eyes lit up.

'It's a tree!' he exclaimed to his friends.

Encouraged, the man moved his hands in a circular motion, but this time Hari couldn't grasp what he meant. He shrugged and asked his friends to check the nearby trees for anything useful. After a while, they came back, carrying a thick rope they had found hanging from one of the branches. It was too heavy for a single hare to carry, so they each held a part of it in their mouths, working together to lift it and bring it to the pit.

Once they brought the rope, Hari's friends explained what they had learned. The man was a hunter who had accidentally fallen into the very pit he had dug to capture an elephant.

The hunter's face brightened upon seeing the rope. He immediately began making signs with his hands again. Raising his left hand high above his head, his fist closed, he moved the palm of his right hand downwards.

The hares tossed the rope into the pit, but the hunter frowned, shaking his head. He continued making more signs, trying to show that they should hold one end and throw the other down. But when he threw the rope back up, the hares scattered. After a while, they cautiously returned and saw the hunter repeating the same signs. Once again, the hares threw the entire rope into the pit. This went on a few more times until the man gave up.

Hari, unable to understand what the hunter wanted, stared at him with blank eyes. He glanced back at his friends, who were just as puzzled. None of them had any idea how to get their dear friend out of the pit.

Three days passed, and the hares continued to bring food to the hunter and Hari, patiently waiting by the pit. One afternoon, they heard heavy footsteps approaching.

'It must be the hunting squad!' they thought, their ears twitching in fear. They quickly dashed behind a bush and hid.

A group of hunters arrived, setting up traps along the road by the bushes. Hearing the rustling and footsteps above, the hunter began making desperate cries for help. The hunters paused in their tracks. Puzzled, the group started searching for the source of the voices. They scoured the area, peering between trees, checking behind bushes—until they finally stumbled upon the pit, nearly falling in themselves. They moved aside the dead branches covering the pit.

'Hey, Bhalla, is this where you've been hiding? In a pit?' one of the hunters called out.

Bhalla, though relieved to see his companions, remained silent.

'You couldn't wait until the end of the village carnival, huh? And all you've managed to capture is a hare?' another hunter teased, glancing at Hari, who stared back at them with wide, fearful eyes. 'Did you jump in to catch it?'

'I fell in by mistake while setting up a trap for an elephant,' Bhalla explained, his voice strained. 'Please get me out. I've hurt my leg badly.'

'Venturing into the forest alone to capture an elephant, only to end up getting trapped yourself,' laughed a third hunter.

Bhalla's face tightened. The taunts stung, but he swallowed his pride and looked at them, waiting to be helped.

Bhalla's friends picked up the rope lying beside the pit and threw one end down. Seeing this, Hari and his friends realized what the man was trying to say this whole time.

Bhalla tied the rope around his waist and held the rope with his right hand. He signalled to his friends to stop, who were ready to pull him out. Bhalla gestured to Hari to hop onto him. Hari hesitated for a moment before leaping onto Bhalla's left arm. Bhalla carefully shifted Hari onto his lap, giving him a small smile as his friends began pulling them out.

'Shall we capture a few more hares or cook this one?' one of the hunters joked as Bhalla and Hari reached the top.

'We will do no such thing,' Bhalla said firmly, releasing Hari from his grasp. The hare looked at him with wide eyes before running away towards his friends.

'Why did you let it go?' one hunter asked, frowning.

'The hare shared his carrots with me. He's my friend and saviour,' Bhalla replied softly, watching Hari unite with his companions. 'I was a fool not to share food with him when I had the chance.'

'Now, remove all the hare traps. Let's focus on capturing a bigger animal,' indicated Bhalla, looking at his mates.

The hunters exchanged puzzled glances but nodded.

'Help me cover the pit properly,' Bhalla continued. 'We will come back in a few days.'

THE CROWN IN THE WELL

Hari and his friends slowly made their way back to the Whispering Woods, carefully scanning the surroundings for any signs of danger.

That night, Hari couldn't sleep. Though relieved to have made it home safely, the fear of the hunting squad lurking in every corner of the forest weighed heavily on his mind. He tossed and turned, troubled by thoughts of how to keep his friends and himself safe.

Hari was not alone in his worries. The entire forest buzzed with tales of the hunting squad's cruelty. Discontent simmered among the herbivores and smaller carnivores over the free meat policy that blatantly favoured the stronger predators. Sensing the growing unrest, Doxy the fox called for a secret meeting.

It was a warm afternoon. The sun was slowly drifting westwards. Animals of all kinds started arriving for the secret meeting. Each one had been affected by the king's decisions and lived in great fear of the hunting squad's raids.

Lakhan the hare, a close friend of Hari, couldn't contain his frustration any longer. He leapt onto the central rock before Doxy could start the meeting.

'Dear friends,' he began, his voice ringing with determination, 'the mighty carnivores are feasting while we live each day with dread!'

The gathered animals fell silent and turned towards the rock, straining their necks to get a clear view of the hare.

Lakhan shouted, his voice ringing out across the clearing, 'The cruel hunting squad has laid traps throughout the forest and is always hunting us down to drag us off to the farms. A few days ago, we barely escaped, but some of my friends weren't as fortunate.'

He paused, scanning the anxious faces in the crowd. 'We can't keep living like this—on the edge, with danger lurking around every corner, every moment. We must act!'

Doxy raised a paw, signalling Lakhan to be patient. As the animals calmed down, he stepped forward and spoke, 'Thank you all for coming on such short notice. I share the frustration that Lakhan so passionately expressed. Some of you might wonder how a carnivore like me could possibly understand your plight,' he began, his gaze sweeping over the crowd. 'But let me assure you—I hunt for my food; I don't take free meat from the king.'

Doxy paused, letting his words settle. 'No one is truly safe in this forest. Today, it's hares, rabbits, cows, bulls, ducks, and pigs. Tomorrow, it could be foxes or any other creature the king deems expendable. I see the injustice as clearly as you do—the fear that grips you every time you step out to forage. This is not the way of a fair ruler. It's the mark of a tyrant.'

'We miss freely hopping along the beach in the mornings and resting under the trees in the afternoons,' said a deer, echoing the sentiments of many forest inhabitants.

'I miss rolling in the mud without looking over my shoulder,' complained a wild boar. 'Now, I have to rush back home after gathering food. My skin is a mess with insect bites.'

'I heard they serve food three times a day on the farms,' a snake hissed thoughtfully.

'What good is eating three square meals a day when you're only being fattened to become someone else's meal?' retorted a wise old tortoise from behind.

All the animals nodded in agreement.

'I heard that every Sunday, the king's band plays music for them. Last week, the king himself sang,' Doxy remarked with a mocking smile.

'Trust me, you don't want to hear him sing,' chimed in a bull who had escaped from one of the farms. 'A bear yawning sounds better. After I heard that awful singing, I knew I had to get out of there.'

'The conditions on the farms are terrible,' the bull

continued. 'Sure, they feed you, but you're locked up. There's barely enough room to stretch, and you are punished if you sleep even a little too long.'

'We need to act fast before we all end up in those farms,' a monkey interjected.

'As residents of Nallamalla, we deserve the freedom to sleep as long as we want, stretch under the open sky, and breathe fresh air—not the stale air of the farms,' Doxy declared passionately. 'We should be free to roll in the mud, swim in the lake, and bask in the sun. These are our fundamental rights, as outlined in the forest charter, since the beginning of this forest.'

He paused and gazed at the animals before continuing with renewed intensity. 'These illegal farms must be shut down immediately! Every animal has the right to roam freely in our forest. No more free meat!'

'No more free meat,' the animals shouted in unison.

'King Maheesha must resign. He must go,' Doxy responded.

'King Maheesha must go,' the animals roared back.

Hari approached Doxy and whispered, 'I have a plan,' his voice barely audible amid the noise.

Doxy turned towards him sharply, drawing the attention of everyone around.

'What is your plan?' Doxy asked eagerly, stepping closer to the nervous hare.

Hari glanced around cautiously. 'It's a secret,' he replied softly.

He took a deep breath and then added, 'But I need a volunteer.'

Doxy approached Chimpu, the chimpanzee, known for his skill with the sling. Without hesitation, Chimpu agreed to help Hari.

The next morning, Hari woke up early, eager to set his plan in motion. Meanwhile, King Maheesha was lounging in his opulent den when Detective Crow flew in and landed quietly on a nearby rock. The king had enlisted a team of detectives to monitor the forest's activities, and Detective Crow, sharp-eyed, was one of his most trusted agents.

'Welcome, Detective Crow! What brings you here so early?' Maheesha greeted warmly.

'O mighty king, may victory be yours. I apologize for visiting you so early in the morning, but the matter is urgent,' Detective Crow replied, bowing her head respectfully.

Maheesha turned his gaze away slightly, a subtle signal for her to continue.

'I have reason to believe the herbivores, along with a few carnivores, are up to something. They held a secret meeting yesterday,' Detective Crow reported.

'What can those grass-eating, slow-chewing creatures possibly do to me?' Maheesha chuckled.

'I overheard them plotting to remove you, Your Majesty. They have a plan,' Detective Crow continued, her voice lowering. 'And Doxy was inciting them.'

Maheesha and his courtiers burst into mocking laughter. 'Let them try,' Maheesha said with a smirk. 'It will be amusing to see what they come up with.'

'Please don't take this lightly,' Detective Crow urged.

'I'll keep an eye out,' Maheesha replied with a chuckle. 'Thank you for the warning.'

Maheesha and his courtiers sniggered as Detective Crow left with a sense of unease, unsettled by how casually the king had dismissed her warning.

Later that evening, Hari sprinted to King Maheesha, panting heavily. He glanced around to make sure no one else was nearby.

'O mighty one, I have urgent news,' Hari gasped, his breath coming in rapid bursts.

'Please hurry; I must prepare for Sunday's performance,' Maheesha responded impatiently.

Struggling to speak between breaths, Hari said, 'You... you need to come with me.'

'A new lion is challenging your authority,' Hari explained, his voice trembling. 'I barely escaped. Two other hares were with me when we were ambushed…but they didn't make it.' Hari's head bowed, his ears drooping in sorrow.

'Another animal trying to be the king?' Maheesha growled. 'This cannot be tolerated. Lead me to this intruder, and I'll deal with him swiftly.'

'The other lion leapt at us from inside the well at the centre of the forest,' Hari continued, his voice trembling. 'I told him we were on our way to meet you, but he attacked us, roaring that he is the new king of Nallamalla.'

Maheesha was even more tickled as he recalled an old tale his grandfather had told him about a clever hare who once tricked his ancestor into jumping into a well.

This hare is trying to use that same trick on me, Maheesha thought. A wry smile spread across his face, recalling Detective Crow's warning. *Is this what those grass-eaters came up with?*

'Is he as formidable as I am?' Maheesha asked curiously.

'He has a build like yours—powerful paws and a majestic mane,' Hari replied, his voice steady despite the fear lurking beneath.

'You must be quite swift to have escaped him,' Maheesha teased with a chuckle. 'Lead the way.'

'You forgot your crown,' Hari reminded.

'You are smart, too,' exclaimed Maheesha, putting on the crown.

How I would deal with the hare once we reached the well, a dark thought lingered at the back of Maheesha's mind.

'Let's take this route—it's faster,' Hari suggested, turning towards an overgrown path that bordered the village. Maheesha followed close behind, his mind preoccupied with thoughts of what he would do with the hare once this was all over.

I could throw him into the well... No, perhaps I should send him to the farm instead, Maheesha mused, chuckling internally at the hare's pitiful attempt at deception.

Distracted by his ideas of revenge, the lion strode ahead of Hari. Suddenly, Maheesha vanished into the ground with a loud thud. Hari skidded to a stop, his heart pounding as he peered into the pit into which Maheesha had fallen.

A gentle smile spread across his face as he watched the mighty lion making desperate attempts to climb out. It was the same pit that Hari had fallen into a few days ago.

Hari shook his head, his ears twitching in amusement. The path he had chosen was rarely used by animals because of the many hidden traps. But, preoccupied with his vengeful thoughts, Maheesha had failed to notice the danger beneath his paws.

Chimpu, hiding behind a bush, cautiously approached the pit to check on the trapped lion. He jumped back, hearing Maheesha's roar as the lion frantically clawed at the walls to get out.

Hari caught Chimpu's eye and silently pointed to a hunter slumped on a branch of a nearby tree, back against the trunk. He was fast asleep.

'A lion falling into a pit didn't wake this man. Does the sky have to fall?' Chimpu remarked jokingly.

'No, but a stone might,' Hari replied with a sly smile.

Chimpu readied his slingshot and took careful aim. The stone struck the hunter on the shoulder, jerking him awake and nearly knocking him off the branch.

Bhalla the hunter rubbed his eyes and looked down. When he saw the lion trapped in the pit, he was both shocked and amused. He quickly called his fellow hunters.

'We aimed for an elephant, but it seems the forest gods have blessed us with a lion,' Bhalla chuckled. 'Let's take him to the circus.'

Together, they bound Maheesha tightly and secured his mouth with a muzzle. As he struggled, Maheesha realized the gravity of his mistake in taking that path.

This hare has outwitted me, Maheesha thought ruefully. *I had planned to throw him into the well, but now look at me.*

Before it got dark, the hunters swiftly began leading the lion towards the village. From their hiding spot behind a bush, Hari and Chimpu watched the scene unfold, feeling relieved.

As the sun began its descent beyond the horizon, Maheesha's courtiers returned to his den after an evening stroll through the forest.

'He's missing,' one of them murmured.

Despite a thorough search of the surrounding area, there was no trace of Maheesha. One lion suggested that perhaps the lion king had gone hunting to keep his skills sharp. They spent the night combing through Nallamalla, even venturing into areas Maheesha was unlikely to frequent.

Soon, the morning sun slowly crept over the horizon. The birds, fully awake, filled the air with their chirping. Monk, however, was still slumbering on a high branch of the mango tree. The cool morning breeze drifting off the lake gently brushed against his fur, taking him deeper into the embrace of a dream.

Monk glided leisurely across the lake on a small wooden board. Ripples formed around, shimmering with an orange hue before dissolving back into the water. As he approached the centre of the lake, a massive wave suddenly surged towards him at alarming speed. Before he could react, the wave crashed over him, pulling him under.

Monk found himself submerged in a dark well, gasping for breath and struggling to stay afloat. He glanced up, searching desperately for a way out, when a wooden crown descended from the sky, landing gently atop his head.

Monk woke up with a jerk. He sighed in relief, realizing he was still on the branch. The meaning of the dream eluded him, leaving him unsettled. As he rubbed his eyes and peered down, he noticed Maheesha's courtiers resting beneath the tree. A wolf woke up and stared at Monk, its eyes filled with deep sadness.

Monk raised an eyebrow and asked, 'What are you doing under the mango tree? Did the king cut off your free meat allowance and put you on a fruit diet?'

'No, Mr Monk, King Maheesha is missing. We've been searching for him all night,' the wolf explained.

'Maybe the king just wanted some quiet time to himself,' Monk suggested with a shrug.

'He's never done that before,' the wolf pleaded with a naive look on his face. 'We need your help.'

Monk hesitated, then decided to join the search. Though he had distanced himself from Maheesha and disapproved of how the lion mistreated smaller animals, he was still the king of the forest. He was unable to shake off the lingering memory of his dream as they combed through the forest.

By afternoon, news of King Maheesha's disappearance had spread like wildfire, prompting Monk to call an urgent assembly of anxious animals. He stood before the gathered crowd, calm and composed, as more creatures trickled in, murmuring with concern.

'By now, I'm sure you've all heard about King Maheesha's disappearance,' Monk began, his voice unruffled but firm. 'We are still actively searching for him, and I urge everyone to refrain from indulging in rumours or jumping to conclusions. Our search efforts will continue, and we remain hopeful for his swift and safe return.'

'He jumped into the well,' Hari said softly.

'What?' Monk asked, his eyebrows raised.

Hari climbed onto a nearby rock and raised his voice. 'King Maheesha jumped into the well.'

Monk shook his head in disbelief. 'You're lying. Why would King Maheesha jump into a well?'

But Hari stood his ground. 'I saw it with my own eyes. You can ask Chimpu. He was there, too.'

Chimpu, who had been quietly standing at the edge of the assembly, stepped forward. 'Yes, I saw it happen,' he confirmed. 'Before he jumped, he was agitated—talking about another lion inside the well that challenged him.'

Hari and Chimpu led the animals to the well. They all peered into the well. There, drifting quietly on the surface of the water, was Maheesha's wooden crown.

The dream I had is indeed real, Monk thought as he peered into the well. *The king, along with his crown, jumped into the well.*

Everyone fell silent. Stepping back from the well, the animals wide eyed, exchanged glances, unable to believe it. The king's courtiers stood frozen in shock, staring into the water below.

'Did he really jump into the well?' a deer asked in a hushed voice.

'He must have,' a wolf replied grimly. 'The lion always wore his crown wherever he went.'

'What happens now?' a bull wondered.

Before anyone could answer, the animals slowly began to disperse—some in sorrow, others in quiet relief. Monk quietly stepped away from the well and started walking towards the lake.

After the crowd had dispersed, Chimpu turned to Hari and asked, 'How did the crown end up in the well?'

'The king jumped into the well,' Hari joked with a grin.

'Come on, tell me the truth,' Chimpu insisted, his eyes narrowing.

'The hunters tossed Maheesha's crown aside before hauling him away,' Hari replied calmly. 'I picked it up and threw it into the well to make it look like he jumped.'

'That was very clever. But how did you know there was a trap?' Chimpu asked, his curiosity piqued.

'That's a tale for another day!' Hari smiled, his gaze drifting towards the flickering lamplight in the village.

For the first time in a long while, the forest felt safe and free from the dread of many months. The reality that Maheesha was no longer around them brought a sense of relief to many animals. They could finally roam without the fear of being chased or captured by the hunting squad.

I AM A FOX

'Why are you crawling so slowly?' asked Shashi, the mother rabbit.

'Shh, silence,' warned her young son, Shashaka, glancing back with a serious expression.

Curious, Shashi crept up behind him and whispered, 'What is it?'

Without a word, Shashaka pointed ahead. Shashi squinted, trying to understand what he was showing her.

'What is it?' she repeated, puzzled.

'There's a cage!' Shashaka whispered, his face tense as he curled up close to his mother.

Shashi placed a gentle paw on his shoulder and spoke in a calming tone. 'That cage was left behind by the hunting squad when they abandoned the forest. No more Maheesha, no more hunting squad. We're safe now.'

Shashaka's ears perked up, and he jumped with joy.

'The hunting squad may be gone, but we still need to watch out for snakes and foxes,' Shashi reminded him gently as they continued their food search.

The forest was slowly adjusting to life without Maheesha and the cruel hunting squad. The herbivores and even some of the carnivores felt a wave of relief. They celebrated, hailing Hari the hare as a hero. Convinced that the lion king had leapt into the well, everyone praised Hari for tricking him. Yet only Hari and Chimpu knew the truth—that Maheesha had been captured by hunters.

With Maheesha gone, his ministers and courtiers had scattered to different corners of the forest, leaving the animals without a ruler or any form of governance. Monk the monkey was on his favourite mango tree by the lake. Gazing at the still water, he pondered the uncertain future that lay ahead for them. Questions about the next king, the fate of the animal farms, and the free meat policy weighed heavily on everyone's minds.

With no king to lead, the election committee swiftly convened and appointed Doxy as the guardian king until the next elections in two years. With no other lion or viable contender in sight, Doxy's rise to power seemed inevitable. At last, Doxy's long-held dream of becoming king was fulfilled.

Upon taking the oath, Doxy wasted no time in implementing sweeping changes. Addressing the gathered animals, he spoke with his head held high.

'My fellow creatures of the forest, today marks an important moment in our history. As your guardian king, I stand here with humility and respect. For too long, we've lived in the shadow of fear and oppression. But today, my friends, that all changes.'

Doxy continued, his voice steady and resolute. 'I stand here not as a ruler, but as a servant of the forest. Today, I uphold the values of freedom and equality. From this moment, all animal farms are abolished, and our brothers and sisters in them are free. Today also marks the end of the free meat policy.'

The animals erupted in cheers, chanting, 'No more free meat!'

Doxy paused, allowing their voices to settle, before continuing. 'Let us not stop there, because true freedom knows no boundaries. Let us put aside our differences and embrace the diversity that makes our forest strong. Together, we can build a future where every creature can thrive, regardless of species or status.'

'For the future!' they chanted in response to Doxy's speech.

The next day, jubilant celebrations spread throughout the forest. The herbivores rejoiced in Doxy's rise to power, the abolition of meat farms, and their newfound freedom from Maheesha's oppressive reign. Laughter and cheers filled the air as animals danced in celebration.

Amidst the festivities, a small lion cub—thin, hungry, and with scruffy fur—timidly emerged from behind a cluster of shrubs. He cautiously stepped forward, and the lively revelry came to an abrupt halt as all eyes turned towards him. Unaware of the reason for the celebration, the cub stared back, bewildered by the sudden attention.

'Are you thinking what I'm thinking?' Ballooka the bear asked a buffalo who was grazing with his head down.

'I've got too much grass between my jaws to ponder,' the buffalo replied, chewing slowly. 'What's between your jaws?'

'Never mind,' Ballooka shrugged, turning his attention to Doxy, who was now staring thoughtfully at the young lion cub.

Deep in thought, Doxy remarked, 'What should we do with the cub?'

'Exactly,' Ballooka nodded. 'What should we do with the cub?'

An excitable murmur broke out among the gathered animals. The cub, son of the lion king Maheesha, had no one left to care for him. Maheesha's queen had died giving birth, and the king—drunk with power—had driven away all other lions from the forest to secure his rule. However, with Maheesha gone, the cub was an orphan.

'We could put him up for adoption,' suggested a monkey, scratching his head.

'Or send him to his relatives in the adjacent forest,' the owl offered.

The assembly fell silent. Each animal was deep in thought, searching for a solution. Finally, Doxy raised his voice to share his thoughts on the cub.

'Consider this,' he began, his tone cautious yet firm. 'What if this cub grows up to be like his father? What if he reinstates the free meat policy and brings back the farms?'

The assembly grew quiet, Doxy's words sinking in as the weight of his warning jolted them. A hush fell over the crowd as the terrible memories of Maheesha's reign flashed through their minds and gripped them with fear.

'I know the cub looks innocent, but we cannot take any chances with him,' Doxy continued, his voice serious. Doxy noticed the puzzled faces around him.

'What's your plan, then? Are you suggesting we lock up the cub?' a fox asked.

'Or throw him out of the forest?' a snake hissed from the back.

'No,' Doxy said firmly. 'We will raise the cub ourselves, so he doesn't grow up to be like his father. If the cub grows among us, he will understand us and our ways.'

The animals exchanged curious glances, murmuring in excitement. 'A lion growing up among us!'

'Who will take care of him?' asked the buffalo, finally lifting his head.

'I will,' quipped Doxy confidently.

Without hesitation, the animals unanimously agreed, placing their trust in Doxy to raise the cub.

Doxy took the lion cub under his wing, bringing him to live among the foxes. At first, the cub was shy and withdrawn, but the young foxes welcomed him warmly and never treated him as different. Gradually, he blended in and became part of the pack. He learned to hunt, chasing rabbits, squirrels, chipmunks, and birds around the forest. Over time, he grew up eating and hunting just like the foxes. He even started to act like them, adopting their playful, agile nature.

Yet, despite his fox-like habits, the cub—now grown—retained the unmistakable appearance of a lion. His thick, golden mane stood in stark contrast to the slender, grey coats of his fox friends.

Meanwhile, a young fox named Khikhi joined the pack on their hunting adventures. Full of boundless energy and curiosity, Khikhi always had a question on his lips. Every moment was a chance to learn, and he eagerly explored the world, seeking answers to everything that puzzled him. Few could satisfy his endless curiosity, but that never stopped him from raising his paw to ask.

As a pup, Khikhi would flick his tail while watching the other foxes and ask his mother, 'Why do we have these? Do they help us run faster—or are they just for swatting flies?'

Later, watching a kingfisher nestled over its eggs, Khikhi tilted his head and mused, 'Why can't we lay eggs like that? It must be nice to sit on them all day and wait for them to hatch.'

And when the clouds turned auburn around the setting sun, Khikhi would squint up and wonder aloud, 'Why does the sun turn red at dusk? Is he blushing?'

Khikhi's parents and friends grew tired of his endless questions. Even the other animals in the forest would avoid him, overwhelmed by his strange questions for which they had no answers.

One day, Khikhi approached the young lion while they were near the lake.

'Why are you among the foxes? You look different,' Khikhi asked with his paw near his mouth.

When the young lion looked at his reflection on the lake's surface, his broad shoulders and thick mane caught his eye. He turned to look at Khikhi. The cub looked at his

reflection in the lake's surface, then turned to Khikhi.

'I have four legs, two eyes, and a nose…just like you,' he said quietly.

Before Khikhi could respond, their friends called them back to play, pulling the lion into their games.

At the next grand assembly, Doxy the fox addressed the gathering, his head held high. 'In the past two years, our forest has flourished under my guardianship. We rid ourselves of the cruel hunting squad and dismantled the animal farms. Normalcy has returned to Nallamalla, and we are thriving once again. It gives me great pleasure to announce that the population of herbivores has doubled.'

Doxy paused as the animals burst into applause.

Once the cheers began to fade, he continued, his voice brimming with pride. 'On this momentous occasion, I am honoured to present to you, Veera.'

Veera the young lion, though shy, stepped forward and stood beside Doxy. His fox friends gathered behind him, howling proudly. In an attempt to mimic them, the young lion let out a soft roar that came out sounding funny. The animals burst into laughter.

It was neither a howl nor a roar, so they decided to call it a 'rowl'.

Encouraged by the laughter, Veera 'rowled' again,

resulting in another wave of laughter from the gathering of delighted animals.

'Veera is gentle, compassionate, and friendly. He is one of us,' Doxy declared proudly.

The animals cheered to the sound of Veera's 'rowling'. It brought much joy to the thousands of animals across the forest. The Whisparrot network spread the word beyond their borders, reaching neighbouring forest communities.

However, the news also reached a renegade pack of wolves led by Sambha. Sambha was a fierce and ruthless hunter, and together with his pack, they mercilessly hunted other animals. Feared for their lightning-fast ambushes, Sambha's wolves could appear before their prey in the blink of an eye, leaving no time for them to react. Known for his deep disdain for authority, Sambha had always been in rebellion against the kings.

The next day, Sambha addressed his pack, his eyes gleaming with malice. 'Nallamalla is the one place we've never been able to plunder. We were always repelled by King Maheesha, who protected it. But today, it's under the guardianship of Doxy—a fox who turned a lion into one of his own,' he said with a smirk. 'This is our chance to fulfil that long-held desire. Tomorrow, we strike at dawn. We'll take as much as we can carry. Be prepared—attack, plunder, leave.'

The wolves repeated their pledge in unison, 'Attack, plunder, leave,' their howls rumbling through the forest.

The next day, Sambha and his pack launched a lightning attack on the Nallamalla Forest. Many deer fell prey to their ruthless onslaught as the wolves advanced. Even the wild buffaloes swimming in the lake were attacked.

The crows and eagles circled in the sky, following the chaos the wolves had unleashed as they ventured deeper into the forest. Sensing danger at the sight of the birds, Monk the monkey swiftly ordered his friends to climb as high into the trees as they could.

As the wolves continued their rampage, they crossed the lake and reached the den where Doxy lived along with Veera. Witnessing the approaching danger, Veera's friends fled, scampering away to safety. But Veera, loyal to Doxy who had raised him, stood his ground and remained by his side.

Sambha, the leader of the wolves, looked at Veera and sneered, 'So, you are the animal with the funny "rowl". Why are you living with the foxes? You're a lion.'

'I'm a fox,' Veera insisted, turning his face away defiantly.

The wolves laughed and taunted him, 'You're a lion, no matter what you think!'

Veera's frustration flared. 'I am a fox. I am a fox,

period!' he snapped, digging his paws into the ground and letting out a soft 'rowl'.

As the wolves advanced towards him, Veera swiftly darted away, evading them and rushing towards his fox friends, who were hiding behind the bushes. The wolves, undeterred, rounded up Doxy. Fear flickered in Doxy's eyes as the wolves closed in on him.

Doxy's heart pounded as Sambha surrounded him, each step like the slow drip of water after a storm. His paws shook as Sambha's piercing gaze held him in place.

'So, you're the one who turned a lion into a fox and crowned yourself king.' Sambha leaned in close, his breath hot against Doxy's ear.

Trembling, Doxy curled his tail tightly around himself, uncertain what the wolf would do to him. 'Please,' he whispered, barely recognizing his voice.

'A true king evokes fear and commands respect,' Sambha taunted, his voice dripping with scorn. 'Look at you—shivering before me like a frightened little mouse.'

Facing Doxy, Sambha struck him hard over the head with his left paw, sending the fox collapsing to the ground, his front legs stretched forward.

'Please, spare me! You can be the king of this forest!' Doxy pleaded desperately, his voice trembling.

Sambha let out a cruel laugh. 'King?' he sneered. 'I don't need a throne. We wolves bow to no one—we bring kings to their knees.'

With a fierce display of aggression, Sambha raised his paws and struck Doxy repeatedly on his legs. The fox cried out in agony and fell to the ground, writhing in pain. His front legs became numb. 'You are not a normal king anymore! You are a crippled king,' Sambha sneered, bursting into laughter as he led his pack away.

As Veera and his friends waited in hiding, Khikhi looked at him and asked gently, 'You look confused. What's wrong?'

Veera kept his head down, his voice low and uncertain. 'I'm a fox…right? But the wolves say I'm a lion.'

Khikhi paused, studying his friend's face. 'I've never seen a lion before,' he said, resting a paw over Veera's. 'But…you do look different.' As the wolves' howls faded into the distance, the forest lay scarred by the surprise attack. Animals emerged from their hiding places, quivering with uncertainty. Broken branches, trampled grass, injured animals, and scattered remains marked the wolves' path. Whispers spread among the survivors. Would the wolves return? And who would protect them if they did?

VEERA'S ROAR

As the wolves retreated from the Nallamalla Forest, they left a trail of destruction in their wake. Carcasses lay scattered across the woodlands that had once teemed with life. The vibrant lakeside now stood eerily deserted—except for a few crocodiles basking on the beach under the warmth of the winter sun, indifferent to the devastation around them.

Veera and his fox friends returned after making sure the wolves had left. They were horrified to find Doxy writhing in pain. His front legs had been broken at the knees, and he was unable to stand. The sight of the once agile and energetic Doxy, lying helpless, stunned them into silence. They gathered around him, watching solemnly as Doxy cried in pain.

The injured fox, enduring immense pain, looked up at Veera and spoke in a strained voice. 'I'm sorry I didn't tell you this before, Veera, you are the son of the mighty lion king, Maheesha, who was elected as the king and ruled this forest before me. But Maheesha favoured the carnivores who voted for him, rewarding their loyalty with free meat and neglecting the herbivores and smaller animals. Fearing you might follow in his footsteps, I decided to raise you among the foxes.'

Doxy paused, his body trembling as the pain in his legs

grew sharper. 'I had hoped to rule the forest, even after you grew up,' he continued. 'My greed has now left Nallamalla without a powerful king and made me a cripple.'

Veera stepped back. Struggling to come to terms with the unexpected revelation about his father and his identity, he stared in silently.

The fox's voice shook with guilt. 'Please, forgive me, Veera,' he said, eyes downcast. 'You were always meant to be a lion.'

Overwhelmed by the gravity of the situation, surrounded by foxes with downcast faces, Veera turned and bolted in the direction of the village. His fox friends ran after him, worried, but he shrugged them off and kept running. His heart pounded and his legs ached, but he kept sprinting through the forest. He did not stop until he reached the edge of a large hill at the forest's perimeter. Exhausted, he curled under the shade of a tree. He decided to rest there for the day.

By the time Veera woke up, the sun had already set, and the full moon hung high in the eastern sky. As he rubbed his eyes, Veera noticed shadowy figures surrounding him. His heart raced with fear, and he tried to run, but a pride of young lions had encircled him. They studied him with curious eyes.

'He looks like a lion,' one of them murmured, 'but he doesn't act like one.'

A few young male lions approached Veera, and they playfully tried to prod him. Veera flinched and closed his eyes. Just as they moved closer, a lioness named Lini stepped forward, blocking their path.

'Looks like he's terrified. Let him calm down,' Lini said calmly, addressing the other lions. 'Please back off.'

However, they mischievously tried to poke Veera while moving away. Lini's patience snapped, and she let out a sudden, fierce roar. Veera, already jittery with nervousness, became even more terrified hearing Lini's roar.

As the rest of the pride backed off, Lini approached Veera slowly, her steps soft and unthreatening.

'What's your name?' she asked gently. 'Why are you out here all alone, and why are you so afraid of us?'

Veera stammered, still bewildered, 'I...I'm Veera. A fox. I'm scared of lions...but you seem...you seem kind.'

Lini chuckled softly. 'You're a lion. Just look at yourself—you look exactly like one of us.'

'That's what the wolves said, too. But I was raised by a fox... I grew up with them,' replied Veera.

Lini's eyes remained fixed on him, listening attentively.

'I always thought I was a fox,' Veera continued, his voice quieter now. 'But then Doxy, the one who raised me, revealed that I'm the son of Maheesha.'

'So, you're the son of Maheesha—the mighty lion king who once ruled Nallamalla,' Lini said softly. 'That explains why you ended up with the foxes.'

Veera looked down with his brow furrowed. 'Now, I don't know who I am. Am I supposed to become a lion? What do I do?'

Lini stepped closer, gently placing her paw over Veera's. 'You're clearly a lion on the outside,' she said softly. 'But now it's time to become one on the inside. Others have defined your identity till now. It's time you discover what you really are.'

Listening to her words, Veera lifted his head and met Lini's reassuring gaze.

'Join us,' she said with a playful wink. 'We'll help you become the lion you're meant to be.'

Veera hesitated, then spoke softly. 'But...please ask your friends not to tease me.'

Lini smiled, shaking her head gently. 'I can't promise that. You'll have to learn to handle them on your own.'

Veera joined the pride, eager to learn and live as a lion.

Under Lini's patient guidance, he began training to hunt and survive the lion's way.

One night, Lini approached Veera. 'Get ready,' she said. 'Tonight, you'll be leading the hunt.'

Veera was caught off guard. 'Me?' he mumbled.

Lini grinned. 'Time to show your skills. Lion-up.'

Veera reluctantly stood up and followed Lini. They moved quietly through the shadows. The forest was alive with the sounds of the night. They came across a colony of hares, fast asleep under the bushes. Veera instinctively began creeping towards them. But before he could get too close, Lini reached out and stopped him.

'You might be leading, but Lini decides what to hunt,' teased one of the young lions with a mischievous grin.

Lini shot him a sharp look. 'We hunt bigger prey. Hares are too small for us,' she said.

'I've never hunted anything bigger than a hare,' Veera admitted, glancing nervously at Lini.

'Well, get ready. Today, you're going after a bull.' In the distance, a massive bull stood near the water's edge, looking around. The bull lost its way home and was searching for its herd.

They approached the bull in silence. Veera felt a mix of fright and excitement as he signalled to the other lions, directing them to surround the bull from all directions. They closed in without making any noise. As they were close enough to attack, the lions looked at Veera. Veera summoned all the courage and made a giant leap, latching onto the bull. Immediately, others jumped in and restrained the animal.

'Not bad for your first attempt,' Lini remarked with a smile as the pride feasted on their prey.

With every hunting trip, Veera's confidence grew. The lions had warmed up to him, particularly enjoying his efforts to master the lion's roar. But despite his best attempts, he still 'rowled', and the pride couldn't help but laugh.

Soon, after a month of intense learning, Veera became adept at leading the hunts and skilfully guiding the pride. Though he had made great strides in the subject, the majestic roar continued to elude him, and the other lions were always bemused at his attempts. Only Lini found it earnest, and she couldn't help but develop a fondness for Veera's innocent charm.

One day, as the pride of young lions strolled through the forest, basking in their time together, the atmosphere suddenly shifted. The ground trembled with the sound of hurried footsteps, and the air grew thick with dust. Deer, buffaloes, and other animals surged past, fleeing in panic.

'Who are they running from? We're the ones who should be making them run,' Lini remarked, watching the fleeing animals.

Among the fleeing animals, Veera spotted his old fox friends. He swiftly intercepted them. The foxes, though breathless and panicked, felt a wave of relief upon seeing their old friend—who had now fully transformed into a lion.

'Greetings, Veera. It's been a long time,' Khikhi panted, struggling to catch his breath.

'Why are you all running? What's happening?' Veera asked, noticing the fear etched on their faces.

'Sambha and his pack of wolves have launched another attack. All the animals are fleeing to save themselves,' one of the foxes explained, still panting. 'Veera, you should come with us. They're vicious...cruel.'

For a moment, Veera considered joining the fleeing animals, but then he remembered who he was. He was a lion. Resolutely, he chose to stand his ground.

One of the younger lions, noticing Veera's fox friends, teased them, 'Did you learn that "howl" from these foxes?'

The pride erupted in laughter. Though a bit embarrassed, Veera couldn't help but chuckle along with them.

Veera's fox friends fled deep into the forest, while the lions stood relaxed, ready for the wolves.

Moments later, a cloud of dust rose behind the bushes lining the road. The lions swiftly took their positions, with Veera standing firm at the centre. The wolves drew closer, their teeth dripping with blood, their eyes narrowed with cruel intent.

Veera took a deep breath, summoning all his strength. He unleashed a powerful, majestic roar that echoed through the forest. It was Veera's first roar! The sound shook the nearby trees, sending birds scattering into the sky. Even Veera's fellow lions were momentarily stunned, awestruck by the sheer majesty of it. What a momentous occasion for the first roar!

Upon hearing the roar, the wolves stopped in their tracks. Their eyes turned to Sambha as he stepped forward. They had not expected to face the lions and were clearly taken aback.

'Listen, Sambha,' Veera declared, stepping forward. 'You won't attack this forest as long as I'm here. Turn back now and save yourselves.'

'Don't you remember what you said a month ago?' Sambha mocked. 'Back then, you claimed you were a fox.'

Veera stood tall, his voice steady. 'I am the son of the great lion king Maheesha. I heard he chased you off when you attacked Nallamalla a few years ago. Or have you forgotten?'

Sambha's eyes narrowed. 'First, you say you're a fox, and now you proclaim to be a lion. We're not afraid of you, Veera. Step aside or face the consequences.'

In a flash, Veera leapt forward, striking Sambha with a powerful swipe of his right paw. Sambha flew, crashing hard into a nearby rock.

'Now, who do you think I am?' Veera roared, his voice echoing through the forest.

'I get it, I get it—you're a lion!' Sambha cried out, squirming in pain. He struggled to stand.

Witnessing the pitiful state of their leader, the other wolves snarled and advanced to attack Veera. But before they got closer, the lions, who had been silently watching, leapt forward towards the wolves. Together, they let out a powerful roar, shaking the ground beneath them. Feeling outpowered and terrified, the wolves swiftly turned around and fled for their lives. Sambha slowly limped behind them.

The lions were impressed by Veera's first roar—grand and perfectly timed. Word spread quickly through the forest, and the animals were grateful to him for saving them from the ruthless wolves.

A few days later, Veera visited Doxy with his pride. Doxy had come to terms with his new reality and now spent most of his time resting in his den, lovingly cared for by the other foxes. Word of Veera's arrival spread quickly, and soon, all the animals gathered there, including his old fox friends.

'O mighty lion, son of Maheesha,' a monkey pleaded, stepping forward. 'You are a true example of selflessness. Despite how we treated you, you saved us from the wolves. We humbly request that you be the king of Nallamalla.

This forest needs the protection of a strong leader like you.'

Despite displaying immense strength, Veera replied humbly, 'It was my duty as a resident of this forest. But I cannot be the king.'

Doxy, his voice heavy with remorse, spoke up. 'Veera, you've shown all the qualities of a great king. We deeply regret keeping you from realizing your true nature, but this forest needs a leader—and you are the best fit. No one else could protect Nallamalla the way you have.'

Veera, casting a glance at Lini with a spark in his eyes, declared, 'To be king, I need a queen.'

Lini, with a playful smirk, raised an eyebrow. 'Is that your way of proposing?'

Veera bent down, his voice softening. 'I'm not sure if you'd accept...but will you be my queen?'

In an instant, the forest erupted into a spontaneous chorus as all the animals shouted in unison, 'Please accept!'

With a warm smile, Lini looked into Veera's eyes and said, 'Yes.'

Veera, filled with joy, let out a colossal roar. The ground quaked under the power of his regal voice, the sound echoing through the entire forest.

'That's Veera's second roar!' one of the lions remarked.

A wave of happiness swept through the assembly. They danced and celebrated long into the night. The forest erupted in cheers and jubilation as they honoured the union of Veera and Lini. This marked the beginning of a new chapter for Nallamalla under their leadership.

EPILOGUE

KHIKHI'S DILEMMA

Is roaring enough to rule the forest? Veera recalled Khikhi's words during his coronation.

Realizing there might be more to ruling the forest than simply roaring, he entrusted Queen Lini with running the forest and left to study leadership at Kingship Academy—founded by the wise old lion, Madusa, the former ruler of Nallamalla.

Meanwhile, Khikhi, realizing few in the forest could answer his endless questions, turned to nature itself. Through quiet observation, he began uncovering clues on his own—like predicting rain by watching the birds. 'See how they fly low?' he'd tell his puzzled friends. 'That means the rain's coming.'

After years of relying on Maheesha's free meat, many carnivores had lost their hunting instincts. A special school was started to retrain the foxes, including Khikhi and his friends. One morning on their way to the school, they spotted Queen Lini approaching Doxy's den with a piece of meat. She placed it gently before him and offered a quiet, respectful roar—a gesture Veera had begun as a tribute to the fox who once sheltered him as a cub. While Veera studied at Kingship Academy, Lini carried on the tradition in his absence.

'A queen came to meet Doxy,' Khikhi whispered, wide-eyed. Watching Lini and the old fox share quiet words, he felt a growing reverence.

If a king and queen visit him, Doxy must be truly special, he thought.

One of his friends tried explaining Veera's story, but Khikhi was too mesmerized to listen.

The next morning, Khikhi was nowhere to be found. His friends searched everywhere. Thinking he'd gone early to school, inspired by Veera's visit, they hurried to the school, but he wasn't there.

They finally found him, sitting with his front legs stretched out, face lifted to the sky, eyes closed in silent meditation, attempting to imitate the crippled fox.

'Are you skipping class?' one asked.

'I've received a divine message,' Khikhi whispered. 'I no longer need to hunt.'

'Are you learning from Doxy?'

'No,' he replied, smiling serenely.

Before they could question him further, he waved them off, his smile growing wider as they left.

By the fourth day, Khikhi's smile had faded. Pale and weak, he remained beside Doxy, refusing food.

Concerned, the head teacher from the hunting school came to check on him.

'Khikhi,' he asked gently, 'why haven't you been attending school?'

Khikhi opened his eyes. 'Master, you said to look for signs—whether hunting or not.'

'Yes, I did,' the master replied patiently.

'Well, I've received my divine message,' Khikhi said proudly.

Curious, the master inquired, 'What is it?'

Khikhi responded, 'Every day, the lioness brings meat for Doxy. Isn't that a sign? Isn't that a divine message?'

The master nodded thoughtfully. 'Yes, Khikhi, it is indeed a divine message. But tell me, what lesson have you gathered from it?'

With a glimmer of pride, Khikhi replied, 'I am simply imitating Doxy, waiting for my piece of meat to arrive.'

The master smiled gently. 'Tell me, Khikhi, why have you chosen to imitate the crippled fox rather than the generous lion? Why did you choose to imitate the one being fed, rather than the one who feeds?

The question utterly perplexed Khikhi. *Why didn't I think of that?* he wondered, eyes wide, tail twitching with deep realization.

A few moments later, Veera slowly emerged from behind the bushes with a piece of meat in his mouth. Having returned from the Kingship Academy, he came to meet Doxy. Khikhi's gaze followed Veera as he walked over to Doxy. He noticed, for the first time, the contentment and joy in Veera's eyes as he offered a small piece of meat to the fox.

Veera turned towards Khikhi and placed a small piece of meat in front of him.

'Here. Eat this,' Veera said kindly. 'Lini told me about you.'

But Khikhi shook his head. 'I'll only eat after I've hunted it myself.'

'You can barely swat a fly with that strength!' his friends teased, laughing gently.

Veera chuckled softly. 'Consider this a loan. When you're ready to hunt, you can take over bringing food for Doxy.'

Khikhi hesitated. He tried to rise again but sank back down, defeated. With a reluctant sigh, he leaned forward and took small bites of the meat as his friends watched over him with relief.

Once he had finished, Khikhi rose shakily to his feet, leaning on his friends for support. 'Let's go,' he murmured, his voice soft but determined.

As Khikhi walked back home with his friends, he felt a new sense of purpose. The satisfaction in Veera's eyes had stayed with him, a reminder of what it meant to be a giver.

Veera watched them leave. Then, he turned and walked toward his den, where Lini lay curled up with their newborn son, Singam.

Under Veera's steady rule, Nallamalla Forest flourished. Rainfall became abundant, the rivers swelled with life, and the population thrived in harmony. Amidst it all, Khikhi continued his hunting lessons—though his friends couldn't help but fear that another one of his 'realizations' was just around the corner!

ACKNOWLEDGEMENTS

First, my deepest gratitude to Sadhguru: your yoga and meditation practices helped me stay sane while juggling work, family, and writing.

To Keerthika, my daughter: you patiently listened to my early stories and told me they weren't great—thank you. That honesty pushed me to write better.

To Pranavi, my wife: thank you for repeating things twice while I was lost in thought about the book. You are very patient.

To Prerna Mathur, Managing Editor at Scholastic India: thank you for believing in my work (and for tolerating my endless requests to read just one more story).

To Ashley Kumar, my editor: your feedback took me from being a frog in a well to the top of a mountain with clear view. Thank you for helping this project leap forward.

To Vidisha Ghosh, my proofreader: Thank you for patiently going through every word, every line and making corrections. Don't tell my English teachers!

To Priyankar Gupta, my illustrator: thank you for bringing the stories to life with imagination far beyond mine.

To Nirmala and Vijaya Mohan, my parents: thank you. I owe everything to you.

To my teachers, Aley Kutti (for the well-timed pinch) and Saraswathi (for encouraging us to think independently). You both helped shape the writer in me.

Finally, to Sudha and Ravi: your love and support made me a better person.

And to you, dear reader—thank you for reading. If you liked it, I wrote it. If you didn't…I still wrote it.

ABOUT THE AUTHOR

Karteek Manchala is an engineer in the automotive sector with a deep passion for storytelling. He is the author of *Bhoomi Tantra: The Ways of Soil*, a collection of short stories that inspire readers to view soil not as mere dirt, but as a life-giving force. By blending science with narrative imagination, Karteek invites readers to develop a deeper appreciation for the natural world around us.

His day begins with yoga and meditation, practices that help him navigate life's challenges with calm and clarity. He lives in the Metro Detroit area with his wife, Pranavi, and their daughter, Keerthika. Outside of his professional and creative pursuits, he enjoys gardening, volunteering, and spending quality time with his family.

OTHER BOOKS YOU MAY LIKE!